Times Table Time & Rhyme

Christopher Davies

Copyright © 2017 Christopher Davies

All rights reserved.

ISBN:
ISBN-13:978-1530684113
ISBN-10:1530684110

For Dad, who is a very special and much loved member of our family. Dad's great interest in poetry and other forms of literature has always been a great source of inspiration to me.

Thank you

I would like to thank Merryn for her meticulous editing skills and Brian Davies for his creative support during the development of this book. I would also like to thank Megan for her creative help with the illustrations and Cam for his useful ideas about the Times Table Challenge.

I would like to reserve a special thank you to Pixabay for allowing me to use some of their images.

Finally, I would like to say a massive, big thank you to you the reader for buying this book. I hope you enjoy reading the rhymes and that it helps you to learn your times tables.

CONTENTS

x2	We're going to the Zoo!	2
x3	Fibbing-Fun!	4
x4	Snow Time!	6
x5	Remarkable Ricksy	8
x6	The Easter Bunny	10
x7	Bonfire Night	12
x8	Katie's Cake	14
x9	School Disco Time	16
x10	The Crime of the Century	18
x11	Devon Heaven	20
x12	Sue's Sports Day	22

Message to children, parents, carers, grandparents & teachers

I hope you have hours of fun reading these rhymes and learning your times tables together. When reading, please read **'the numbers'** in the following way:

"**One 2 is 2** – We're going to the Zoo!"
"**Two 2's are 4** – Hear those hippos snore!"
"**Three 2's are 6** – Chimps performing tricks!"

This will help to keep the pace of the rhyme quite snappy and slightly quicker than if you use, "1 times 2 equals 2, 2 times 2 equals 4…". (The rhymes will also scan better using the first method.)

You can use this book in many ways. You can read it on your own or with a partner. If reading with a partner, sometimes you could read **just** the **numbers** and your partner could read the **corresponding rhyme**. For example you read, "One 2 is 2," and they read, "I'm going to the zoo!" Then you read, "Two 2's are 4," and they read, "Hear those hippos snore!" This will help you focus on the number pattern of the times table. After a while swap over and let your partner read the numbers and you can read the corresponding rhyme. Before long you will know your times tables off by heart!

Times Table Challenge

Ready to challenge yourself? When you are trying to recall your times table from memory, the rhymes can be used to help you to remember the correct answer. For example, if you are stuck on 3 x 2 = ? Your reading partner can read the next line of the rhyme - "Chimps performing tricks!" You will then know that the answer you need rhymes with 'tricks'. Using the rhyme as clues will make learning your times tables more fun and interactive. This will also help speed up your learning!

Challenge Cup & Times Table Champion

At the back of the book you will have the chance to put your times table knowledge to the test! Can you win the Challenge Cup or become a Times Table Champion? I'm sure you can. Good luck!

x2   We're going to the Zoo!

1 x 2 = 2   We're going to the zoo!

2 x 2 = 4   Hear those hippos snore!

3 x 2 = 6   Chimps performing tricks!

4 x 2 = 8   A deadly rattle snake!

5 x 2 = 10   T… TERRIFYING… tiger in its den!

6 x 2 = 12   It even scares my Uncle Melve!

7 x 2 = 14   Fierce, ferocious – looking mean!

8 x 2 = 16   Penguins paddling in frothy stream.

9 x 2 = 18   Elephants squirting, like a car-wash machine!

10 x 2 = 20   The crowd is in a frenzy!

11 x 2 = 22   New-born gorilla, for all to view!

12 x 2 = 24   The 'King of the Beasts' lets out his **ROAR!**

x3   Fibbing-Fun!

Two children in the playground bragging…

1 x 3 = 3   Once I ate a bumble-bee!

2 x 3 = 6   *My monkey can do magic tricks!*

3 x 3 = 9   I can walk a tightrope line!

4 x 3 = 12   *I went to space with my Uncle Melve!*

5 x 3 = 15   I was mascot for the Chelsea team!

6 x 3 = 18   *I had dinner with the Queen!*

7 x 3 = 21   Now that's just silly – I'm not that dumb!

8 x 3 = 24   *I even did cartwheels on the Palace floor!*

9 x 3 = 27   Well, I swam the coast from Dorset to Devon!

10 x 3 = 30   *A SHARK once bit and hurt me!*

11 x 3 = 33   A pirate ship chased me out to sea!

12 x 3 = 36   *I found a TARANTULA in my 'Pick & Mix'!*

x4 Snow Time!

1 x 4 = 4   It's snowing! Get out the door!

2 x 4 = 8   Look! I can nearly skate!

3 x 4 = 12   School plans we gladly shelve!

4 x 4 = 16   The thickest snow there's ever been!

5 x 4 = 20   Snowball fights aplenty.

6 x 4 = 24   Got you Dad! Right on the jaw!

7 x 4 = 28   To the highest hill - we did make.

8 x 4 = 32   Sledging downhill... cries of WHOOP!!

9 x 4 = 36   Jumps and bumps – thrills and tricks!

10 x 4 = 40   Very winter sporty.

11 x 4 = 44   It's getting dark- what a bore!

12 x 4 = 48   Tucked up in bed – our day was great!

x5   Remarkable Ricksy

1 x 5 = 5   Ref! That was a dive!

2 x 5 = 10   No way is that a 'PEN'!

3 x 5 = 15   The worst REF we'd ever seen!

4 x 5 = 20   Jeers and boos aplenty.

5 x 5 = 25   Come on Ricksy - keep the game alive!

6 x 5 = 30   The crowd outraged and shirty.

7 x 5 = 35   He's going to score - we can't survive!

8 x 5 = 40   Their striker stands proud and haughty…

9 x 5 = 45   It's going left! DIVE! DIVE…

10 x 5 = 50   What a save!!! Right nifty!!!

11 x 5 = 55   "Ricksy for England!" rang out the cries.

12 x 5 = 60   Truly, **remarkable** Ricksy!

x6   The Easter Bunny

1 x 6 = 6   Easter eggs and chicks

2 x 6 = 12   Into the woods we delve.

3 x 6 = 18   Searching swiftly into the green...

4 x 6 = 24   Hunting high and on forest floor.

5 x 6 = 30   We're getting COLD and DIRTY!

6 x 6 = 36   All we've found is mud and sticks.

7 x 6 = 42   At last we see THEM - peeping through!

8 x 6 = 48   Big ones, small ones... every shape!

9 x 6 = 54   Fill the basket - more and more!

10 x 6 = 60   Let's keep moving quickly...

11 x 6 = 66   The Easter Bunny's been up to his tricks!

12 x 6 = 72   Delicious eggs for me and you.

x7　　　Bonfire Night

1 x 7 = 7　　　Fireworks fly from heaven!

2 x 7 = 14　　　Orange, purple, red and green.

3 x 7 = 21　　　The bonfire burns like a red-hot sun.

4 x 7 = 28　　　The night Guy Fawkes met with his fate.

5 x 7 = 35　　　Bangers CRACK - like a gun that's live!

6 x 7 = 42　　　Pretty patterns – AAH's! and OOH's!

7 x 7 = 49　　　Rockets soaring – hear them WHINE!

8 x 7 = 56　　　Like a night in the Coventry Blitz!

9 x 7 = 63　　　Sizzling sausages and piping hot tea!

10 x 7 = 70　　　For the cold, it's just the remedy.

11 x 7 = 77　　　Twirling sparklers with Ross and Megan.

12 x 7 = 84　　　It can't be over….???! We want MORE!!

x8 Katie's Cake

1 x 8 = 8   We're going to bake a cake.

2 x 8 = 16   Chocolate sponge with tons of cream!

3 x 8 = 24   Stir the mixture – more and more.

4 x 8 = 32   Eggs and flour - sticky goo!

5 x 8 = 40   Nice but very naughty!

6 x 8 = 48   Place in oven, leave and wait…

7 x 8 = 56   Time to make the icing mix.

8 x 8 = 64   Ping! It's ready! Get the door!

9 x 8 = 72   On the table – finished - PHEW!

10 x 8 = 80   A birthday treat for Katie!

11 x 8 = 88   Blow the candles - wish and wait…

12 x 8 = 96   Pals and presents and party tricks!

x9   School Disco Time

1 x 9 = 9   It's school Disco time!

2 x 9 = 18   Doors are open – in we stream!

3 x 9 = 27   Dancing with my best friend Megan.

4 x 9 = 36   Cool kids doing break-dancing tricks!

5 x 9 = 45   Mrs Jenkins is doing the jive!

6 x 9 = 54   EVERYBODY is on the dance-floor!

7 x 9 = 63   Salah's spinning on one knee!

8 x 9 = 72   Hit sounds blaring - old and new.

9 x 9 = 81   Rock and Hip Hop – so much fun!

10 x 9 = 90   Teachers dancing BLINDLY!

11 x 9 = 99   They're doing the Conga in a great long line!

12 x 9 =108   Dancing the night away, 'til very, very late…

x10 The Crime of the Century

1 x 10 = 10   The crime – who 'dunnit' then?!

2 x 10 = 20   The SWEETIE tin lies EMPTY...

3 x 10 = 30   Mum is getting shirty!

4 x 10 = 40   "Stealing is very naughty!"

5 x 10 = 50   Kids are looking shifty.

6 x 10 = 60   The life of crime is risky!

7 x 10 = 70   Suspects, there are plenty...

8 x 10 = 80   Harry, Will and Katie.

9 x 10 = 90   Dad is looking flighty...

10 x 10 = 100   "Was it HIM!?" they wondered.

11 x 10 = 110   He does love chewy caramels now and again..

12 x 10 = 120   Still unsolved... 'The Crime of the Century'!

x11 Devon Heaven

1 x 11 = 11	Holiday time in Devon.
2 x 11 = 22	Huge waves crashing – what a view!
3 x 11 = 33	Swimming and surfing in the clear blue sea.
4 x 11 = 44	Sea gulls squawking - then up they soar.
5 x 11 = 55	Racing out on a speed-boat ride!
6 x 11 = 66	Dolphins leaping – doing mid-air flicks!
7 x 11 = 77	Slurping ice-creams, this is close to heaven!
8 x 11 = 88	Building castles, then the waves we wait…
9 x 11 = 99	Tide's almost in – going home time!
10 x 11 = 110	"Please Mum! Can we come here again?"
11 x 11 = 121	Holidays in Devon are such great fun!
12 x 11 = 132	So much to see and so much to do!

x12   Sue's Sports Day

1 x 12 = 12   I'm racing my friend Kelve!

2 x 12 = 24   I've never beaten him before.

3 x 12 = 36   Trembling nervously – time just ticks…

4 x 12 = 48   BANG! I'm off! At light-speed rate!

5 x 12 = 60   I'm sprinting VERY quickly!

6 x 12 = 72   He's gaining on me – what shall I do?

7 x 12 = 84   "Get your skates on !" I hear dad roar.

8 x 12 = 96   We're neck and neck – right in the mix!

9 x 12 = 108   I can see the finish – I'm going to faint!

10 x 12 = 120   Nothing left – run out – empty…

11 x 12 = 132   "The 80 metre champion this year, is…. Sue!"

12 x 12 = 144   WOW! I won it! Amazing! COR!!!

Dear Reader

I hope you enjoyed this book. If you did, please leave me a book review on amazon.co.uk. - I would be very interested in hearing from you. Which rhymes and illustrations did you like the best? Has it helped you to learn your times tables? I hope it has!

How much progress have you made? Have you won the 'Challenge Cup' or become a 'Times Table Champion' or 'Super-Champion'?

Keep an eye out for my next book in the series which will be out later in 2018.

Best wishes

Christopher Davies

Challenge Cup

Are you ready to test your times table knowledge and try and win the Challenge Cup? If so, photocopy this grid and see how many you can get right in 10 minutes. The first row is the 10 times table - I have filled in a few answers to help you. Can you **score 132 out of 132** and win the **Challenge Cup**? After each attempt fill in the Date, Time, Score and Target.* (see page 26) **Good luck! You can do it!**

X	1	2	3	4	5	6	7	8	9	10	11	12
10	10	20	30									
5	5	10										
2												
4												
3												
6												
7												
8												
9												
11												
12												
Date				Score				Time			Target	

Tricky Tables Challenge

Are you ready for an even trickier times table challenge? Can you score 100 out of 100 in less than 10 minutes and become a **'Times Table Champion'**?

1) Photocopy this grid & put in 10 numbers from 1 - 12 in a **random** order across the top row. E.g. 2,4,5,3,6,9,7,8,12,11. The first number has been put in for you and the answer 10 x 2 = **20**

2) Give yourself 10 minutes to complete as many as you can – no peeping in the book please!

3) Get some help to check your answers and record your score out of 100 and the time and date.

4) To work out your **Target** for next time, just add on 10. If you scored 45, your new target will be 55. If you score 100 in 10 minutes try and beat your time by 10 seconds and so on. If you score 100 out of 100 in less than 8 minutes you will become a … **'Times Table Super-Champ'**?!

x	2									
10	20									
5										
2										
4										
3										
6										
7										
9										
8										
12										
Date		Score			Time			Target		

Books by Christopher Davies

If you would like to buy or find out about other books written by the author, please check out the Author's Page for Christopher Davies on amazon.co.uk

Printed in Great Britain
by Amazon